PERFORMANCE ASSESSMENT TEACHER'S GUIDE

8

Printed in the U.S.A.

ISBN 978-0-544-14768-3

7 8 9 10   0928   22 21 20 19 18 17 16 15

4500549734   C D E F G

Approaching Performance Assessments with Confidence

By Carol Jago

The best assessments reflect best practice. Rather than asking students to perform artificial tasks, assessments worth giving include texts worth reading and tasks worth doing. Ideally, time spent on such formative assessments shouldn't be time lost to instruction but rather an opportunity both for students to demonstrate what they have learned as well as a chance for additional practice.

Malcolm Gladwell estimates in his book *Outliers* that mastering a skill requires about 10,000 hours of dedicated practice. He argues that individuals who are outstanding in their field have one thing in common—many, many hours of working at it. Gladwell claims that success is less dependent on innate talent than it is on practice. Now I'm pretty sure that I could put in 10,000 hours at a ballet studio and still be a terrible dancer, but I agree with Gladwell that, "Practice isn't the thing you do once you're good. It's the thing you do that makes you good."

Not just any kind of practice will help students meet English Language Arts Standards, though. Effective practice needs to focus on improvement. That is why this series of reading and writing tasks begins with a model of the kind of reading and writing students are working towards, then takes them through practice exercises, and finally invites them to perform the skills they have practiced.

Once through the cycle is only the beginning. You will want your students to repeat the process several times over until close reading, supporting claims with evidence, and crafting a compelling essay is something they approach with confidence. Notice that I didn't say "with ease." I wish it were otherwise, but in my experience as a teacher and as an author, writing well is never easy.

I hope you find these assessment tools a valuable, seamless addition to a standards-aligned curriculum.

Unit 1 Argumentative Essay
Teen Culture

Unit 2 Informative Essay
Shaping the Earth

Unit 3 Literary Analysis
Common Ground

Unit 4 Mixed Practice
On Your Own

Teen Culture

STEP 1 ANALYZE THE MODEL

Should all U.S. students be required to speak at least one language besides English?

Page 5
Close Read

Student answers should demonstrate comprehension and draw evidence from the text. They may cite the author's belief that it is important for Americans to join "the cross-cultural conversation" and the fact that there is great demand for foreign language skills in law enforcement and intelligence agencies.

Page 7
Discuss and Decide

As students discuss whether they should be required to learn a second language, remind them to cite textual evidence.

Page 9
Discuss and Decide

As students discuss the strengths and weaknesses of Adeline's argumentative essay, remind them to cite textual evidence.

Page 10
Terminology of Argumentative Texts

Accept reasonable responses that demonstrate comprehension of the terms and their application to the texts.

STEP 2 PRACTICE THE TASK

Should students be required to stay in school until they are 18?

Page 13
Discuss and Decide

As students discuss the reasoning in Marissa's letter and the possible consequences of her leaving school, remind them to cite textual evidence.

Page 15
Close Read

1. Student answers should demonstrate comprehension and draw evidence from the text. They may cite lower earnings, higher unemployment, and lower job satisfaction as reasons for staying in school.

2. Student answers should demonstrate comprehension and draw evidence from the text. They may mention that states requiring students to stay in school until they graduate are still facing high dropout rates as a reason for why raising the minimum age doesn't lead to higher graduation rates.

Page 16
Respond to Questions on Step 2 Sources

1. Accept responses that demonstrate comprehension and draw evidence from the source. Reputable newspapers check their sources and the source of the graph data is very credible, so it is likely that this information is accurate. The interview and letter contain personal opinions and may not be accurate.

2. Prose Constructed-Response

Scoring Notes: Use the rubric to evaluate student responses. Responses may include but are not limited to:

- The graph with information sourced from the U.S. Department of Education provides the most credible evidence that earning income is directly related to graduating from high school.

- The radio interview with Education Advocate Missy Remiss presents a strong argument for the importance of a high school diploma.

2	The response gives sufficient evidence of the ability to evaluate the credibility, completeness, relevancy, and/or accuracy of the information and sources.
1	The response gives limited evidence of the ability to evaluate the credibility, completeness, relevancy, and/or accuracy of the information and sources.
0	A response provides no evidence of the ability to evaluate the credibility, completeness, relevancy, and/or accuracy of the information and sources.

3. Prose Constructed-Response
Scoring Notes: Use the rubric to evaluate student responses. Responses need to cite evidence from the argument given in Source 1, the letter from Marissa to her grandmother, in which Marissa expresses the great need to help out her family financially.

2	The response gives sufficient evidence of the ability to evaluate the credibility, completeness, relevancy, and/or accuracy of the information and sources.
1	The response gives limited evidence of the ability to evaluate the credibility, completeness, relevancy, and/or accuracy of the information and sources.
0	A response provides no evidence of the ability to evaluate the credibility, completeness, relevancy, and/or accuracy of the information and sources.

Pages 18–20
Planning and Prewriting
Review and critique students' planning documents; offer feedback as needed.

Pages 21–22
Argumentative Essay
Scoring Notes: Use the rubric to evaluate student responses.

	Development of Ideas	Organization	Clarity of Language	Language and Conventions
4	The response addresses the prompt and shows effective and comprehensive development of the claim using text-based evidence, clear and convincing reasoning, and/or description.	The response demonstrates coherence and clarity, a logical organization that includes an introduction and conclusion, and a logical progression of ideas.	The response establishes and maintains an effective style, including precise language, descriptive words and phrases, transitional words and phrases, and domain-specific vocabulary.	The response demonstrates a command of standard English conventions consistent with effectively edited writing.
3	The response addresses the prompt and shows effective development of the topic using text-based evidence, reasoning, and/or description.	The response demonstrates some logical organization and includes an introduction and conclusion.	Some descriptive words, as well as some linking words and phrases, are used to express ideas with clarity.	The response demonstrates a command of standard English conventions, although there may be some minor errors in grammar and usage.

	Development of Ideas	Organization	Clarity of Language	Language and Conventions
2	The response addresses the prompt and shows some development of the topic but fails to use text-based evidence, reasoning, and/or description.	The response demonstrates little logical organization and includes either an introduction or a conclusion.	Few descriptive words, as well as a few linking words and phrases, are used and ideas are not expressed as clearly as possible.	The response demonstrates a command of standard English conventions, although there are major errors in grammar and usage.
1	The response does not directly address the prompt, shows no development of the topic, and fails to use text-based evidence, reasoning, and/or description.	The response demonstrates little logical organization and fails to include either an introduction or a conclusion.	No descriptive words or linking words and phrases, are used and ideas are not expressed with clarity.	Errors in grammar and usage create confusion of meaning.
0	No evidence of the ability to write an argumentative essay.			

STEP 3 PERFORM THE TASK

Should individuals be prosecuted for statements made on social media?

Page 25
Close Read

Student answers should demonstrate comprehension and draw evidence from the text. They may cite a limitation of the proposed law, such as isolated incidents not being considered as cyberbullying.

Page 26
Close Read

Student answers should demonstrate comprehension and draw evidence from the text. They may cite that it is more difficult for the victim to avoid the bully in cases of cyberbullying.

Page 28
Close Read

Student answers should demonstrate comprehension and draw evidence from the text. They may include the author's belief that "the Senators want to punish people for not allowing NY citizens to join their online clubs."

Page 29
Discuss and Decide

As students discuss which fact from the sheet most strongly demonstrates that cyberbullying is a serious problem, remind them to cite textual evidence.

Page 30
Respond to Questions on Step 3 Sources

1. Accept responses that demonstrate comprehension and draw evidence from the source. Students will need to carefully evaluate the evidence that supports the opinions presented in the interview and article to determine whether they are reliable sources. The fact sheet is published by a source that is unknown to most readers; it should be researched, but is probably a reliable source of information.

2. Prose Constructed-Response

   Scoring Notes: Use the rubric to evaluate student responses. Responses may include, but are not limited to:

   • Cyberbullying is a crime and needs to be prosecuted appropriately.

   • People are overreacting to cyberbullying and new legislation would interfere with our First Amendment rights.

   • Cyberbullying can include any hurtful statements on the Internet made against an individual.

2	The response gives sufficient evidence of the ability to evaluate the credibility, completeness, relevancy, and/or accuracy of the information and sources.
1	The response gives limited evidence of the ability to evaluate the credibility, completeness, relevancy, and/or accuracy of the information and sources.
0	A response provides no evidence of the ability to evaluate the credibility, completeness, relevancy, and/or accuracy of the information and sources.

Pages 31–32
Argumentative Essay
Scoring Notes: Use the rubric to evaluate student responses.

	Development of Ideas	Organization	Clarity of Language	Language and Conventions
4	The response addresses the prompt and shows effective and comprehensive development of the claim using text-based evidence, clear and convincing reasoning, and/or description.	The response demonstrates coherence and clarity, a logical organization that includes an introduction and conclusion, and a logical progression of ideas.	The response establishes and maintains an effective style, including precise language, descriptive words and phrases, transitional words and phrases, and domain-specific vocabulary.	The response demonstrates a command of standard English conventions consistent with effectively edited writing.
3	The response addresses the prompt and shows effective development of the topic using text-based evidence, reasoning, and/or description.	The response demonstrates some logical organization and includes an introduction and conclusion.	Some descriptive words, as well as some linking words and phrases, are used to express ideas with clarity.	The response demonstrates a command of standard English conventions, although there may be some minor errors in grammar and usage.
2	The response addresses the prompt and shows some development of the topic but fails to use text-based evidence, reasoning, and/or description.	The response demonstrates little logical organization and includes either an introduction or a conclusion.	Few descriptive words, as well as a few linking words and phrases, are used and ideas are not expressed as clearly as possible.	The response demonstrates a command of standard English conventions, although there are major errors in grammar and usage.

	Development of Ideas	Organization	Clarity of Language	Language and Conventions
1	The response does not directly address the prompt, shows no development of the topic, and fails to use text-based evidence, reasoning, and/or description.	The response demonstrates little logical organization and fails to include either an introduction or a conclusion.	No descriptive words or linking words and phrases are used and ideas are not expressed with clarity.	Errors in grammar and usage create confusion of meaning.
0	No evidence of the ability to write an argumentative essay.			

Shaping the Earth

STEP 1 ANALYZE THE MODEL

How do nature and humans shape the earth?

Page 37
Discuss and Decide

As students discuss which text structure would be more helpful in discussing how a car works, remind them to cite textual evidence.

Page 39
Discuss and Decide

As students discuss which type of cause-effect organization is used in the essay and why it is an effective way to present information on erosion, remind them to cite textual evidence.

Page 41
Discuss and Decide

As students discuss whether or not a cause-and-effect organization could be used with this topic, and, if so, which model would work best, remind them to cite textual evidence.

Page 42
Terminology of Informative Texts

Accept reasonable responses that demonstrate comprehension of the terms and their application to the texts.

STEP 2 PRACTICE THE TASK

What are the effects of an earthquake?

Page 45
Close Read

Student answers should demonstrate comprehension and draw evidence from the text. They may cite reasons for what causes movement in the Earth's continents, such as how they slide over the planet's molten mantle.

Page 46
Discuss and Decide

As students discuss which details in the blog help them picture the events described, remind them to cite textual evidence.

Page 47
Discuss and Decide

As students discuss the most destructive effect of the Loma Prieta earthquake, remind them to cite textual evidence.

Page 48
Discuss and Decide

As students discuss which details from the insurance claim help them better understand the scope and cost of an earthquake's destructiveness, remind them to cite textual evidence.

Page 49
Respond to Questions on Step 2 Sources

1. c.

2. c.

Page 50
Respond to Questions on Step 2 Sources

3. b.

4. c.

5. b.

Page 51
Respond to Questions on Step 2 Sources

6. Prose Constructed-Response

Scoring Notes: Use the rubric to evaluate student responses. Responses may include but are not limited to:

- The main idea and supporting details of "If You Travelled to Gondwana…"

2	The response gives sufficient evidence of the ability to cite evidence to support arguments and/or ideas.
1	The response gives limited evidence of the ability to cite evidence to support arguments and/or ideas.
0	A response gets no credit if it provides no evidence of the ability to cite evidence to support arguments and/or ideas.

7. Prose Constructed-Response

Scoring Notes: Use the rubric to evaluate student responses. Responses may include but are not limited to:

- Information about the effects of earthquakes in the insurance claim.

2	The response gives sufficient evidence of the ability to evaluate the credibility, completeness, relevancy, and/or accuracy of the information and sources.
1	The response gives limited evidence of the ability to evaluate the credibility, completeness, relevancy, and/or accuracy of the information and sources.
0	A response provides no evidence of the ability to evaluate the credibility, completeness, relevancy, and/or accuracy of the information and sources.

Pages 52–54
Planning and Prewriting

Review and critique students' planning documents; offer feedback as needed.

Pages 55–56
Informative Essay

Scoring Notes: Use the rubric to evaluate student responses.

	Development of Ideas	Organization	Clarity of Language	Language and Conventions
4	The response addresses the prompt and shows effective and comprehensive development of the claimusing text-based evidence, clear and convincing reasoning, and/or description.	The response demonstrates coherence and clarity, a logical organization that includes an introduction and conclusion, and a logical progression of ideas.	The response establishes and maintains an effective style, including precise language, descriptive words and phrases, transitional words and phrases, and domain-specific vocabulary.	The response demonstrates a command of standard English conventions consistent with effectively edited writing.
3	The response addresses the prompt and shows effective development of the topic using text-based evidence, reasoning, and/or description.	The response demonstrates some logical organization and includes an introduction and conclusion.	Some descriptive words, as well as some linking words and phrases, are used to express ideas with clarity.	The response demonstrates a command of standard English conventions, although there may be some minor errors in grammar and usage.

	Development of Ideas	Organization	Clarity of Language	Language and Conventions
2	The response addresses the prompt and shows some development of the topic but fails to use text-based evidence, reasoning, and/or description.	The response demonstrates little logical organization and includes either an introduction or a conclusion.	Few descriptive words, as well as a few linking words and phrases, are used and ideas are not expressed as clearly as possible.	The response demonstrates a command of standard English conventions, although there are major errors in grammar and usage.
1	The response does not directly address the prompt and shows no development of the topic and fails to use text-based evidence, reasoning, and/or description.	The response demonstrates little logical organization and fails to includes either an introduction or a conclusion.	No descriptive words or linking words and phrases are used and ideas are not expressed with clarity.	Errors in grammar and usage create confusion of meaning.
0	No evidence of the ability to write an informative essay.			

STEP 3 PERFORM THE TASK

How do volcanoes affect people and environments?

Page 59
Close Read

Student answers should demonstrate comprehension and draw evidence from the text. They may cite possible answers to the title's question, such as "there is no accurate count."

Page 61
Close Read

Student answers should demonstrate comprehension and draw evidence from the text. They may cite reasons why it is important to know that the soil in southern Italy is unusually poor, such as how volcanic eruptions have made the soil around Naples more fertile.

Page 62
Discuss and Decide

As students discuss the effect of volcanoes on Mauna Loa, remind them to cite textual evidence.

Page 63
Respond to Questions on Step 3 Sources

1. b.

2. c.

3. b.

4. Prose Constructed-Response

   Scoring Notes: Use the rubric to evaluate student responses. Responses may include but are not limited to:

   • Information about how volcanic eruptions have improved the natural landscape of Mauna Loa.

2	The response gives sufficient evidence of the ability to cite evidence to support arguments and/or ideas.
1	The response gives limited evidence of the ability to cite evidence to support arguments and/or ideas.
0	A response gets no credit if it provides no evidence of the ability to cite evidence to support arguments and/or ideas.

Page 64
Respond to Questions on Step 3 Sources

Prose Constructed-Response

5. Scoring Notes: Use the rubric to evaluate student responses. Responses may include but are not limited to:

   • Information about how the eruption of Mount Vesuvius affected the region around Naples.

2	The response gives sufficient evidence of the ability to cite evidence to support arguments and/or ideas.
1	The response gives limited evidence of the ability to cite evidence to support arguments and/or ideas.
0	A response gets no credit if it provides no evidence of the ability to cite evidence to support arguments and/or ideas.

6. Prose Constructed-Response

Scoring Notes: Use the rubric to evaluate student responses. Responses may include but are not limited to:

• Information about why it is important to define what a volcano is.

2	The response gives sufficient evidence of the ability to cite evidence to support arguments and/or ideas.
1	The response gives limited evidence of the ability to cite evidence to support arguments and/or ideas.
0	A response gets no credit if it provides no evidence of the ability to cite evidence to support arguments and/or ideas.

Pages 65–66
Informative Essay

Scoring Notes: Use the rubric to evaluate student responses.

	Development of Ideas	Organization	Clarity of Language	Language and Conventions
4	The response addresses the prompt and shows effective and comprehensive development of the controlling idea using text-based evidence, clear and convincing reasoning, and/or description.	The response demonstrates coherence and clarity, a logical organization that includes an introduction and conclusion, and a logical progression of ideas.	The response establishes and maintains an effective style, including precise language, descriptive words and phrases, transitional words and phrases, and domain-specific vocabulary.	The response demonstrates a command of standard English conventions consistent with effectively edited writing.
3	The response addresses the prompt and shows effective development of the topic using text-based evidence, reasoning, and/or description.	The response demonstrates some logical organization and includes an introduction and conclusion.	Some descriptive words, as well as some linking words and phrases, are used to express ideas with clarity.	The response demonstrates a command of standard English conventions, although there may be some minor errors in grammar and usage.

	Development of Ideas	Organization	Clarity of Language	Language and Conventions
2	The response addresses the prompt and shows some development of the topic but fails to use text-based evidence, reasoning, and/or description.	The response demonstrates little logical organization and includes either an introduction or a conclusion.	Few descriptive words, as well as a few linking words and phrases, are used and ideas are not expressed as clearly as possible.	The response demonstrates a command of standard English conventions, although there are major errors in grammar and usage.
1	The response does not directly address the prompt, shows no development of the topic, and fails to use text-based evidence, reasoning, and/or description.	The response demonstrates little logical organization and fails to include either an introduction or a conclusion.	No descriptive words or linking words and phrases are used and ideas are not expressed with clarity.	Errors in grammar and usage create confusion of meaning.
0	No evidence of the ability to write an informative essay.			

Common Ground

STEP 1 ANALYZE THE MODEL

How do authors use their own style to express common themes?

Page 71
Discuss and Decide

As students review Jocelyn's side notes with a partner and discuss the unique elements of the writer's style that she notes, remind them to cite textual evidence.

Page 73
Discuss and Decide

As students discuss with a partner the way the unique aspects of Giovanni's style affect Jocelyn's interpretation of the poem, remind them to cite textual evidence.

Page 74
Terminology of Literary Analysis

Accept reasonable responses that demonstrate comprehension of the terms and their application to the texts.

STEP 2 PRACTICE THE TASK

How can poetry create common ground?

Page 76
Close Read

Student answers should demonstrate comprehension and draw evidence from the text. They may describe how the words in lines 10–14 convey the idea that the statue is the "Mother of Exiles," such as the fact that she is taking on the role of a caretaker.

Page 79
Discuss and Decide

As students discuss with a small group whether the newspaper article is effective in explaining the historical events surrounding the poem, remind them to cite textual evidence.

Page 80

Respond to Questions on Step 2 Sources

1. a.

2. d., e., h.

Page 81

Respond to Questions on Step 2 Sources

3. c.

4. d., e., h.

Page 82

Respond to Questions on Step 2 Sources

5. Prose Constructed-Response

> **Scoring Notes:** Use the rubric to evaluate student responses. Responses may include but are not limited to:
>
> • Information about the events that inspired Emma Lazarus to write her poem.

2	The response gives sufficient evidence of the ability to gather, analyze, and integrate information within and among multiple sources of information.
1	The response gives limited evidence of the ability to gather, analyze, and integrate information within and among multiple sources of information.
0	A response gets no credit if it provides no evidence of the ability to gather, analyze, and integrate information within and among multiple sources of information.

6. Prose Constructed-Response

> **Scoring Notes:** Use the rubric to evaluate student responses. Responses may include but are not limited to:
>
> • Information about what the initial reaction of the people of the United States to the Statue of Liberty was.
>
> • Analysis of how Emma Lazarus's poem changed the way the statue was viewed.

2	The response gives sufficient evidence of the ability to gather, analyze, and integrate information within and among multiple sources of information.
1	The response gives limited evidence of the ability to gather, analyze, and integrate information within and among multiple sources of information.
0	A response gets no credit if it provides no evidence of the ability to gather, analyze, and integrate information within and among multiple sources of information.

7. Prose Constructed-Response

Scoring Notes: Use the rubric to evaluate student responses. Responses may include but are not limited to:

- Analysis of how the Statue of Liberty goes on speaking to immigrants today.

2	The response gives sufficient evidence of the ability to gather, analyze, and integrate information within and among multiple sources of information.
1	The response gives limited evidence of the ability to gather, analyze, and integrate information within and among multiple sources of information.
0	A response gets no credit if it provides no evidence of the ability to gather, analyze, and integrate information within and among multiple sources of information.

Pages 83–84
Planning and Prewriting

Review and critique students' planning documents; offer feedback as needed.

Pages 85–86
Literary Analysis

Scoring Notes: Use the rubric to evaluate student responses.

	Development of Ideas	Organization	Clarity of Language	Language and Conventions
4	The response addresses the prompt and shows effective and comprehensive development of the controlling idea using text-based evidence, clear and convincing reasoning, and/or description.	The response demonstrates coherence and clarity, a logical organization that includes an introduction and conclusion, and a logical progression of ideas.	The response establishes and maintains an effective style, including precise language, descriptive words and phrases, transitional words and phrases, and domain-specific vocabulary.	The response demonstrates a command of standard English conventions consistent with effectively edited writing.

	Development of Ideas	Organization	Clarity of Language	Language and Conventions
3	The response addresses the prompt and shows effective development of the topic using text-based evidence, reasoning, and/or description.	The response demonstrates some logical organization and includes an introduction and conclusion.	Some descriptive words, as well as some linking words and phrases, are used to express ideas with clarity.	The response demonstrates a command of standard English conventions, although there may be some minor errors in grammar and usage.
2	The response addresses the prompt and shows some development of the topic but fails to use text-based evidence, reasoning, and/or description.	The response demonstrates little logical organization and includes either an introduction or a conclusion.	Few descriptive words, as well as a few linking words and phrases, are used and ideas are not expressed as clearly as possible.	The response demonstrates a command of standard English conventions, although there are major errors in grammar and usage.
1	The response does not directly address the prompt, shows no development of the topic, and fails to use text-based evidence, reasoning, and/or description.	The response demonstrates little logical organization and fails to include either an introduction or a conclusion.	No descriptive words or linking words and phrases are used and ideas are not expressed with clarity.	Errors in grammar and usage create confusion of meaning.
0	No evidence of the ability to write a literary analysis.			

STEP 3 PERFORM THE TASK

How do we respond to historic events?

Page 90
Close Read

Student answers should demonstrate comprehension and draw evidence from the text. They may cite examples of descriptive details and figurative language that portray the cavalrymen.

Page 92
Discuss and Decide

As students discuss why a military battle might be a good topic for a narrative poem, remind them to cite textual evidence.

Page 94
Close Read

Student answers should demonstrate comprehension and draw evidence from the text. They may cite the ideas the repeated phrases in lines 1–26 emphasize, such as the dangers that the light brigade must face.

Page 95
Discuss and Decide

As students discuss with a small group the specific details in both the eyewitness account and the narrative poem and why these details might have been chosen by both writers, remind them to cite textual evidence.

Page 96
Respond to Questions on Step 3 Sources

1. Prose Constructed-Response

Scoring Notes: Use the rubric to evaluate student responses. Responses may include but are not limited to:

• Summary of the plot of "The Charge of the Light Brigade."

2	The response gives sufficient evidence of the ability to cite evidence to support arguments and/or ideas.
1	The response gives limited evidence of the ability to cite evidence to support arguments and/or ideas.
0	A response gets no credit if it provides no evidence of the ability to cite evidence to support arguments and/or ideas.

2. Prose Constructed-Response

Scoring Notes: Use the rubric to evaluate student responses. Responses may include but are not limited to:

• Analysis of how the use of rhyme and repetition contribute to the meaning of the poem.

• Analysis of what ideas are emphasized in the poem.

2	The response gives sufficient evidence of the ability to cite evidence to support arguments and/or ideas.

© Houghton Mifflin Harcourt Publishing Company

1	The response gives limited evidence of the ability to cite evidence to support arguments and/or ideas.
0	A response gets no credit if it provides no evidence of the ability to cite evidence to support arguments and/or ideas.

3. Prose Constructed-Response

Scoring Notes: Use the rubric to evaluate student responses. Responses may include but are not limited to:

• Information about what historical facts are in "The Battle of Balaclava" and "The Charge of the Light Brigade."

• Information about the similarities and differences between the historical facts of "The Battle of Balaclava" and "The Charge of the Light Brigade."

2	The response gives sufficient evidence of the ability to gather, analyze, and integrate information within and among multiple sources of information.
1	The response gives limited evidence of the ability to gather, analyze, and integrate information within and among multiple sources of information.
0	A response gets no credit if it provides no evidence of the ability to gather, analyze, and integrate information within and among multiple sources of information.

Pages 97–98
Literary Analysis

Scoring Notes: Use the rubric to evaluate student responses.

	Development of Ideas	Organization	Clarity of Language	Language and Conventions
4	The response addresses the prompt and shows effective and comprehensive development of the controlling idea using text-based evidence, clear and convincing reasoning, and/or description.	The response demonstrates coherence and clarity, a logical organization that includes an introduction and conclusion, and a logical progression of ideas.	The response establishes and maintains an effective style, including precise language, descriptive words and phrases, transitional words and phrases, and domain-specific vocabulary.	The response demonstrates a command of standard English conventions consistent with effectively edited writing.

	Development of Ideas	Organization	Clarity of Language	Language and Conventions
3	The response addresses the prompt and shows effective development of the topic using text-based evidence, reasoning, and/or description.	The response demonstrates some logical organization and includes an introduction and conclusion.	Some descriptive words, as well as some linking words and phrases, are used to express ideas with clarity.	The response demonstrates a command of standard English conventions, although there may be some minor errors in grammar and usage.
2	The response addresses the prompt and shows some development of the topic but fails to use text-based evidence, reasoning, and/or description.	The response demonstrates little logical organization and includes either an introduction or a conclusion.	Few descriptive words, as well as a few linking words and phrases, are used and ideas are not expressed as clearly as possible.	The response demonstrates a command of standard English conventions, although there are major errors in grammar and usage.
1	The response does not directly address the prompt, shows no development of the topic, and fails to use text-based evidence, reasoning, and/or description.	The response demonstrates little logical organization and fails to include either an introduction or a conclusion.	No descriptive words or linking words and phrases are used and ideas are not expressed with clarity.	Errors in grammar and usage create confusion of meaning.
0	No evidence of the ability to write a literary analysis.			

On Your Own

TASK 1 ARGUMENTATIVE ESSAY

Page 115

1. d.

2. Prose Constructed-Response

Scoring Notes: Use the rubric to evaluate student responses. Responses may include but are not limited to:

- Information about the steps Nike took to end its reliance on child labor.

2	The response gives sufficient evidence of the ability to cite evidence to support arguments and/or ideas.
1	The response gives limited evidence of the ability to cite evidence to support arguments and/or ideas.
0	A response gets no credit if it provides no evidence of the ability to cite evidence to support arguments and/or ideas.

3. Prose Constructed-Response

Scoring Notes: Use the rubric to evaluate student responses. Responses may include but are not limited to:

- Two reasons why Nadira Faulmüller hesitates to join boycotts of products made by child labor.

2	The response gives sufficient evidence of the ability to gather, analyze, and integrate information within and among multiple sources of information.
1	The response gives limited evidence of the ability to gather, analyze, and integrate information within and among multiple sources of information.
0	A response gets no credit if it provides no evidence of the ability to gather, analyze, and integrate information within and among multiple sources of information.

Argumentative Essay

Scoring Notes: Use the rubric to evaluate student responses.

	Development of Ideas	Organization	Clarity of Language	Language and Conventions
4	The response addresses the prompt and shows effective and comprehensive development of the claim using text-based evidence, clear and convincing reasoning, and/or description.	The response demonstrates coherence and clarity, a logical organization that includes an introduction and conclusion, and a logical progression of ideas.	The response establishes and maintains an effective style, including precise language, descriptive words and phrases, transitional words and phrases, and domain-specific vocabulary.	The response demonstrates a command of standard English conventions consistent with effectively edited writing.
3	The response addresses the prompt and shows effective development of the topic using text-based evidence, reasoning, and/or description.	The response demonstrates some logical organization and includes an introduction and conclusion.	Some descriptive words, as well as some linking words and phrases, are used to express ideas with clarity.	The response demonstrates a command of standard English conventions, although there may be some minor errors in grammar and usage.
2	The response addresses the prompt and shows some development of the topic but fails to use text-based evidence, reasoning, and/or description.	The response demonstrates little logical organization and includes either an introduction or a conclusion.	Few descriptive words, as well as a few linking words and phrases, are used and ideas are not expressed as clearly as possible.	The response demonstrates a command of standard English conventions, although there are major errors in grammar and usage.

	Development of Ideas	Organization	Clarity of Language	Language and Conventions
1	The response does not directly address the prompt and shows no development of the topic and fails to use text-based evidence, reasoning, and/or description.	The response demonstrates little logical organization and fails to include either an introduction or a conclusion.	No descriptive words or linking words and phrases are used and ideas are not expressed with clarity.	Errors in grammar and usage create confusion of meaning.
0	No evidence of the ability to write an argumentative essay.			

TASK 2 INFORMATIVE ESSAY

Page 127

1. a.

2. d.

3. Prose Constructed-Response

Scoring Notes: Use the rubric to evaluate student responses. Responses may include but are not limited to:

- Information about the role that luck played in Alexander Fleming's discovery of penicillin.

2	The response gives sufficient evidence of the ability to gather, analyze, and integrate information within and among multiple sources of information.
1	The response gives limited evidence of the ability to gather, analyze, and integrate information within and among multiple sources of information.
0	A response gets no credit if it provides no evidence of the ability to gather, analyze, and integrate information within and among multiple sources of information.

Argumentative Essay

Scoring Notes: Use the rubric to evaluate student responses.

	Development of Ideas	Organization	Clarity of Language	Language and Conventions
4	The response addresses the prompt and shows effective and comprehensive development of the claim using text-based evidence, clear and convincing reasoning, and/or description.	The response demonstrates coherence and clarity, a logical organization that includes an introduction and conclusion, and a logical progression of ideas.	The response establishes and maintains an effective style, including precise language, descriptive words and phrases, transitional words and phrases, and domain-specific vocabulary.	The response demonstrates a command of standard English conventions consistent with effectively edited writing.
3	The response addresses the prompt and shows effective development of the topic using text-based evidence, reasoning, and/or description.	The response demonstrates some logical organization and includes an introduction and conclusion.	Some descriptive words, as well as some linking words and phrases, are used to express ideas with clarity.	The response demonstrates a command of standard English conventions, although there may be some minor errors in grammar and usage.
2	The response addresses the prompt and shows some development of the topic but fails to use text-based evidence, reasoning, and/or description.	The response demonstrates little logical organization and includes either an introduction or a conclusion.	Few descriptive words, as well as a few linking words and phrases, are used and ideas are not expressed as clearly as possible.	The response demonstrates a command of standard English conventions, although there are major errors in grammar and usage.

	Development of Ideas	Organization	Clarity of Language	Language and Conventions
1	The response does not directly address the prompt and shows no development of the topic and fails to use text-based evidence, reasoning, and/or description.	The response demonstrates little logical organization and fails to include either an introduction or a conclusion.	No descriptive words or linking words and phrases are used and ideas are not expressed with clarity.	Errors in grammar and usage create confusion of meaning.
0	No evidence of the ability to write an informative essay.			

TASK 3 LITERARY ANALYSIS

Page 140

1. d.

2. a.

3. b.

Page 141

4. Prose Constructed-Response

Scoring Notes: Use the rubric to evaluate student responses. Responses may include but are not limited to:

- A summary and explanation of why there are historical inaccuracies in Longfellow's poem.

- Analysis of why historical accuracy may not have been important to the poet.

2	The response gives sufficient evidence of the ability to cite evidence to support arguments and/or ideas.
1	The response gives limited evidence of the ability to cite evidence to support arguments and/or ideas.
0	A response gets no credit if it provides no evidence of the ability to cite evidence to support arguments and/or ideas.

Page 142
Literary Analysis
Scoring Notes: Use the rubric to evaluate student responses.

	Development of Ideas	Organization	Clarity of Language	Language and Conventions
4	The response addresses the prompt and shows effective and comprehensive development of the claim using text-based evidence, clear and convincing reasoning, and/or description.	The response demonstrates coherence and clarity, a logical organization that includes an introduction and conclusion, and a logical progression of ideas.	The response establishes and maintains an effective style, including precise language, descriptive words and phrases, transitional words and phrases, and domain-specific vocabulary.	The response demonstrates a command of standard English conventions consistent with effectively edited writing.
3	The response addresses the prompt and shows effective development of the topic using text-based evidence, reasoning, and/or description.	The response demonstrates some logical organization and includes an introduction and conclusion.	Some descriptive words, as well as some linking words and phrases, are used to express ideas with clarity.	The response demonstrates a command of standard English conventions, although there may be some minor errors in grammar and usage.
2	The response addresses the prompt and shows some development of the topic but fails to use text-based evidence, reasoning, and/or description.	The response demonstrates little logical organization and includes either an introduction or a conclusion.	Few descriptive words, as well as a few linking words and phrases, are used and ideas are not expressed as clearly as possible.	The response demonstrates a command of standard English conventions, although there are major errors in grammar and usage.

	Development of Ideas	Organization	Clarity of Language	Language and Conventions
1	The response does not directly address the prompt and shows no development of the topic and fails to use text-based evidence, reasoning, and/or description.	The response demonstrates little logical organization and fails to include either an introduction or a conclusion.	No descriptive words or linking words and phrases are used and ideas are not expressed with clarity.	Errors in grammar and usage create confusion of meaning.
0	No evidence of the ability to write a literary analysis.			